Bear's First Christmas

To Paula, editor, mentor, inspiration, and friend
– RK
For Aunt Lin and Uncle Ed
– JL

SIMON AND SCHUSTER
First published in Great Britain in 2007 by Simon & Schuster UK Ltd
Africa House, 64-78 Kingsway, London WC2B 6AH
A CBS company

This paperback edition published in 2008
Originally published in 2007 by Simon & Schuster Books for Young Readers,
an imprint of Simon & Schuster Children's Publishing Division, New York

Text Copyright © 2007 by Robert Kinerk
Illustrations Copyright © 2007 by Jim LaMarche

A CIP catalogue record for this book is available from the British Library

ISBN: 978 1 84738 273 3

Printed in China
10 9 8 7 6 5 4 3 2 1

Bear's First Christmas

Robert Kinerk · Illustrated by Jim LaMarche

SIMON AND SCHUSTER
London   New York   Sydney

It started to snow, and a bear, very young,

Caught two or three flakes on the tip of his tongue.

The coming of snow could mean only one thing.

It meant that the bear had to sleep until spring.

Down a hill, which was steep, past tall cliffs, which were steeper,

The bear trekked through woods that grew deeper and deeper.

He trekked on a path past a lake's sandy shore

And at last found a cave with rough stone for a floor.

At the mouth of the cave the bear noticed a tree

Which struggled to grow where no tree ought to be.

In the view the bear got from the mouth of the cave

The tree looked quite small – but also quite brave.

As he rested his head on his furry, soft paw,

The brave little tree was the last thing he saw.

And then his eyes closed, and on the rough stone

He drifted to sleep, all alone... All alone.

The winter closed in, and days and days passed,
While the wind from the north blew its shivery blast.
On the floor of the forest the snow rose and rose.
And the lakes and the streams and the rivers all froze.
The bear slept, and he dreamt of the coming of spring,
And the showers of rain, and the flowers she'd bring,
And the birds who'd return and who'd swoop through the skies –
But a faraway sound made him open his eyes.

He stepped from his cave and he looked towards a hill.
The shadows he saw all remained very still,
But on wings of the wind, from across the cold ground,
Came the strains of a soft and mysterious sound.

The bear followed the sound, but it stayed very faint
And was lost, by and by, in a crow's harsh complaint.
The crow cawed and cawed, and his caw seemed to say
He needed some help finding food right away.

In all those deep woods there was no one to hear
Except the young bear, and to him it was clear.
He'd have to hike home and then search high and low
For some sort of food for the shivering crow.

Homeward he trudged, with the snow to his knees,
And returned with some honey, a comb from the bees.
The crow pecked his fill of that treat from the bear,
Then he spread his black wings and he took to the air.
He followed the bear, while the moon hid its face
And the stars twinkled cold in the vastness of space.

They came to a bog, where a moose, with his teeth,
Tried to scrape at the ice for the weeds underneath.
He needed some help, which the bear could well see,
So he scraped with his claws till the cold weeds were free.

The moose ate and he ate. When he'd eaten his fill,
He followed the bear and the crow round a hill.
The wind whispered sharp, and the night grew unpleasant
As the bear saw ahead the crushed home of a pheasant.
A branch overhead had let loose loads of snow
That had smashed the bird's home with the force of a blow.

The pheasant had chicks, and
the chicks' cries were pleas
That said to the bear they were
scared they would freeze.
A nod from the bear let the
frightened birds know
They should follow the tracks
that he made through the snow.
Which they instantly did,
on the chance that they might,
With his help, find a place to
be safe through the night.

On the bear trudged till he saw, through more snow,
A lair or a burrow all lit by a glow.
Icicles hung from its top, sharp and bright.
Its sides had a space that was open for light.
And what's this from inside? That wonderful sound!
After all of his trekking, its source had been found!

He crept to the light without making a noise.
In the glow of the light were two girls and two boys.
And pealing from them came mysterious words,
A sound to the bear like the music of birds.

He stood and he stared, and his eyes grew more wide,
For there was a wonderful glowing inside.
A glow with warm rays like the sun at its rise,
A glow cast from faces, a glow cast from eyes.
But a glow most of all from a wonderful tree
That the beasts out of doors were astonished to see.
A tree dressed in lights – each shiny as dew.
What the lights meant, though, no animal knew.

The last of the sounds faded off in the night.
The children inside were led slowly from sight.
Out of doors, the beasts stared as the last embers fell.
They thought and they thought, but they still couldn't tell
What the meaning could be of the music, the lights,
And the gladness inside on this darkest of nights.

But a spark deep inside them gave off that same glow
As they made their way back through the drifts of deep snow.
The bear broke the trail, and he made it so wide,
The moose, who was giving the birds all a ride,
Could quickly and easily follow along
As the birds on his back sang an improvised song,
Which was only "Caw caw!" and merely "Tweet tweet!"
But was shared – and by sharing grew more and more sweet.

The bear showed the pheasants his well-hidden den
To say they could stay until spring came again.
To which all the pheasants were quick to agree,
Though they and the others all stared – at the tree!
At the crooked, the ragged, the struggling tree –
At the tree that was growing where no tree should be.
For the moon in the sky had sent down a bright beam
That touched the tree's branches and made them all gleam.
Almost as if, in the dark of the night,
The tree had been graced by a magical light.

There was room in the cave for the moose and the crow.
They needn't trudge off through the dark and the snow.
Into the cave the bear squeezed with each guest,
And they all settled down to begin their long rest.

They slept, and the tree shed its marvellous light
All through the freezing and long winter night.
It continued to glow when the winter was done
And the earth had been touched by the warmth of the sun.

And the bear, in new treks, knows the light never ends.
It's a knowledge he shares with his wide-roaming friends.
For each friend, though he roams from the others apart,
Carries with him, inside him, that glow in his heart.